RIDDANCE
By Linda McLean

Cast in order of appearance

Kenny Lewis Howden
Claire Carolyn Bonnyman
Frank Neil McKinven

Director Vicky Featherstone
Designer Neil Warmington
Lighting Designer Nigel J. Edwards
Original Music and Sound Nick Powell

Production Manager Alison Ritchie
Company Stage Manager Paul Anders
Technical Stage Manager Louise McDermott
Stage Manager (rehearsals) Jamie Byron

Publicity Photograph Manuel Harlan
Production Photography Sheila Burnett
Set Construction Andy Beachamp
Press Representatives Cameron Duncan PR - 0171 636 3750
Leaflet/Poster Designer Eureka! Graphic Design Ltd

Paines Plough Theatre Company would like to thank the following for their help with this production: Dyson Ltd., Yvonne Milnes, Jake Sharp, Molly Farrell, Sarah Willson (Cello) and Richard Vranch. Wardrobe care by Persil and Comfort courtesy of Lever Brothers Ltd.

THE COMPANY

Linda McLean - Writer

Born in Glasgow, Linda grew up in Castlemilk, Balornock and Cumbernauld. She studied at Strathclyde University and Jordanhill College. After graduating she travelled for a number of years as a teacher and worked in Israel, Yugoslavia, Sweden, Kenya and the USA. She lives with John Ferris and their two children in Winchester.

Her early work had rehearsed readings at the Nuffield Theatre in Southampton. From the encouragement she received there, came *Dearly Held* which was produced at the Ramshorn in Glasgow and *One Good Beating* recently produced by the Traverse Theatre and published by Nick Hern Books. She wrote *Take One Egg* for Radio 4, directed by Patrick Rayner; Corridors, a monologue for Benchtours Theatre Company; and *The price of a Good Dinner*, a monologue for Derby Playhouse Studio. RIDDANCE Is Linda's first production of a full-length play.

She is currently under commission to the Traverse and BBC Radio Scotland.

Paul Anders - Company Stage Manager

Trained at RADA. Recent work includes Company Stage Manager on *Gross Indecency The Impostor* and *Candida* (Plymouth Theatre Royal). For Paines Plough he was CSM or *Crave* (Denmark and Holland tours). He has worked for a variety of theatre companies including Stephen Joseph Theatre Scarborough, Salisbury Playhouse, Almeida Theatre, Royal Court, Young Vic, Apollo/BCC and Shared Experience.

Carolyn Bonnyman – Clare

Theatre includes *Britannia Rules, The Bevellers, Hobson's Choice* (Royal Lyceum) *Dissent* (7:84), *A Christmas Carol* (Compass), *The Seal Wife* (Croydon Warehouse), *Abiding Passions,* (Beltane / Riverside Studios), *Tartuffe, Quelques Fleurs* (Nippy Sweeties), *And A Nightingale Sang...* (Brunton, Byre), *Doctor and the Devils* (Plymouth Theatre Royal) *Politics in the Park* (Tron, Gilded Balloon), *Mary Queen of Scots Got Her Head Chopped Off* (Contact, Manchester), *Loot* (Arches)
Television and Film includes; *Urban Ghost Story* (Living Spirit Pictures), *Heart and Sole* (Tiger Aspect / Channel 4), *Joyride* (BFI / Sidewalk / Channel 4), *Numbertime, Your Cheatin' Heart, Tin Fish, Beatrix Potter* (BBC).
Radio includes *Week Ending, Taking it up the Octave, The Peggers and Creelers, Are You From the Bugle? After Icarus, The Pavilion on the Links,* (Radio 4), *My Mammy and Me, Take Away* (Radio 2)

Jamie Byron - Stage Manager

West End includes *Sunset Boulevard.* Repertory; Chichester Festival Theatre and Sheffield Crucible. Extensive UK and international touring with Triumph Proscenium, E & B, Lee Menzies Ltd, Really Useful Theatre Company, Shared Experience and Theatre De Complicite. Jamie last worked with Paines Plough as Stage Manager on their production of *Crave* by Sarah Kane. After propping for Riddance, he returns to Shared Experience to Stage Manage their international tour of *Jane Eyre*.

paines PLOUGH presents

RIDDANCE

by Linda McLean

Originally commissioned by Paines Plough
First performed at the Traverse Theatre 10 August 1999

Nigel J Edwards - Lighting Designer

Recent works include *The Cosmonaut's Last Message To The Woman He Once Loved In The Former Soviet Union, Crave, Sleeping Around* (Paines Plough), *Shadows, The Mysteries, Roberto Zucco* for the RSC, *Dirty Work, Pleasure* (Forced Entertainment), *House* (an installation), *King Arthur* (Lip Service), *Jenufa* (WNO), *The Maids* for ENO at the Lyric Theatre Hammersmith, *Cleansed* by Sarah Kane at the Royal Court. He has designed the lights for and toured extensively with; *Showtime, Speak Bitterness, Hidden J., Club of no Regrets, Emmanuelle, Enchanted, Marina and Lee* (Forced Entertainment); *Hold Me Down, Baldy Hopkins and Penny Dreadful* (The Right Size); *Waiting For Godot* (Tottering Bipeds) and for Louder Than Words, *Dreamtime* and *Counting Of Years.*

Vicky Featherstone - Director

As Artistic Director of Paines Plough Vicky has directed *The Cosmonaut's Last Message To The Woman He Once Loved In The Former Soviet Union* by David Greig, *Crave* by Sarah Kane, *Sleeping Around* by Stephen Greenhorn, Hilary Fannin, Abi Morgan and Mark Ravenhill, and *Crazyhorse* by Parv Bancil.
She recently directed *The Moment Is A Gift That's Why It's Called The Present* by Abi Morgan, for Prada as part of Milan Fashion Week in June this year and also *Too Cold For Snow* by Michael Wynne in January this year for Prada.
Other theatre includes *Anna Weiss* (Traverse Theatre Edinburgh, won both Fringe First and Scotland on Sunday's Critic's awards), *Kvetch, Brighton Rock* (West Yorkshire Playhouse), *Two Lips Indifferent Red* (Bush Theatre), *The Glass Menagerie, Christmas Carol, My Mother Said I Never Should* (Bolton Octagon), *Women Prefer ...* (Northern Stage).
Other work includes; Script Development Executive for United Film and Television Productions where she created *Where The Heart Is* and developed *Touching Evil.* She is currently Script Development Executive for Granada Television Drama.

Lewis Howden – Kenny

Theatre includes *Fire in the Basement* (Communicado), *Mother Courage, Cutting a Rug* and *Changed Days* (Royal Lyceum), *Macbeth* (Theatre Babel), *Knives in Hens* (Traverse Theatre / Bush), *The Trick is to Keep Breathing* (Tron/Royal Court - Toronto), *Quelques Fleurs* (Nippy Sweeties), *The Crucible, Glengarry Glen Ross* (Arches), *Loose Ends* and *The House Among the Stars* (Traverse Theatre).
Television includes *Taggart, Dr Finlay,* (STV), *Turning World* (CH4/Epicflow), *Rosaleen, Strathblair, Caledonian and Romans* (BBC), *The Chef* (Anglia).
Film includes: *Aberdeen* (Freeway Films), *The Blue Boy* (BBC), *Gare Au Male* (Animula). Radio includes: *Cuba, The Blasphemer* and *Poetry Please* for the BBC.

Louise McDermott - Technical Stage Manager

Trained at Middlesex University in Drama and Technical Theatre. Recent work includes DSM on *Outside the Street* (Gate), ASM on *The Killing Floor* (Bridewell), DSM on *Red Riding Hood and the Wolf* (London Bubble), SM/DSM on *BT National Connections* (Young Vic). Recent national touring productions include CSM on *Romeo and Juliet* (Shakespeare for Kidz) and *Jump to Cow Heaven* (One From The Heart Theatre Company).

Neil McKinven – Frank

Theatre includes; *The Cosmonaut's Last Message To The Woman He Once Loved In The Former Soviet Union* (Paines Plough), *Dissent, Caledonia Dreaming* and *Road* (tours for 7:84), *Fire in the Basement* (Traverse Theatre), *Dead Funny* (Lyceum, Edinburgh), *Widow* (Traverse Theatre), *Afters* (Gilded Balloon, Edinburgh), *The Mark* (Cockpit), *The Ship* (Glasgow Docks), *Underwater Swimming* (New End), *When I Was a Girl I Used to Scream and Shout* (commercial tour). TV includes; *Rab C Nesbitt* (BBC), *The Vet* (BBC), *Degree of Error* (BBC), *Takin' Over The Asylum* (BBC), *Straithblair* (BBC), *The Ship* (BBC), *Taggart* (STV). Film; *The Debt Collector* (Dragon Pictures), *Commission* (Academy Films).

Nick Powell - Original Music & Sound

Nick has been working as a musician since 1990. He has toured and recorded with various bands including *Strangelove* (EMI Records), *Astrid* (Nude Records) and *The Blue Aeroplanes* (Beggars Banquet). He has composed extensively for TV, radio and short films recently for shows on Channel Four, ITV, BBC World Service and Sky One. As Musical Director of Suspect Culture - a theatre company formed in collaboration with Graham Eatough and David Greig - he has scored and been part of the development of eight shows including *Airport, Timeless* and *Mainstream* as well as numerous workshops in Britain and Europe. For Paines Plough he recently composed the music and soundtrack for *The Cosmonaut's Last Message To The Woman He Once Loved In The Former Soviet Union* by David Greig. Through the British Council, he has worked with Teatro De La Jacara in Madrid, Bouge-de-la and The Max Factory. He is one half of the duo *OSKAR* whose debut album will be released in the next few months. Most recently *OSKAR* composed the music and sound for *The Moment Is A Gift That's Why It's Called The Present* by Abi Morgan and performed live for Prada as part of Milan Fashion Week in June '99.

Neil Warmington - Designer

Neil gained a First Class BA Hons degree in fine art, before completing a post-graduate Theatre design course at Motley. Recent theatre credits include: Desire *Under the Elms, Jane Eyre* (Shared Experience), *Crazyhorse*, (Paines Plough), *Don Juan, Taming of the Shrew* (English Touring Theatre), *Family, Passing Places* (Traverse), *Dissent, Angels in America* (7:84), *The Glass Menagerie, Comedians* (Royal Lyceum, Edinburgh), *Life is a Dream, Fiddler on the Roof* (West Yorkshire Playhouse), *The Duchess of Malfi* (Bath Theatre Royal), *Henry V* (Royal Shakespeare Company), *Much Ado About Nothing* (Queen's, London), *Life of Stuff* (Donmar Warehouse), *Much Ado about Nothing, Waiting For Godot* (Liverpool Everyman), *The Tempest* (Contact, Manchester), *Women Laughing* (Watford), *Troilus & Cressida* (Opera North), *Oedipus Rex* (Connecticut State Opera), Neil Recently designed Glasgow's 1999 Year of Architecture Launch, and his awards include 3 TMA Awards for best design (*Jane Eyre* 1998), The Linbury Prize for Stage Design, and The Sir Alfred Munnings Florence Prize for painting.

INTRODUCTION

It is only by truly encouraging writers to push the boundaries of theatre and their own ideas that great drama will ever emerge.

Paines Plough has no particular theatrical style - our work is dictated by the individual requirements or tone of the different plays. For an audience, this means that no two plays or indeed experiences of our work will ever be the same. This makes the company unique. We place our trust in the vision of the writer, which is kept firmly at the heart of the company.

RIDDANCE is testament to this. Linda McLean was my first commission when I arrived at Paines Plough. The development of this play has taken two years and shows Linda's development from a writer of promise to one of, I believe, great talent. She constantly strives for a deeper theatrical meaning and unnervingly edits and refines her work, seeking clarity and maximum dramatic effect.

I am very proud of the development of RIDDANCE and hope it speaks to you, the audience, in the way we believe it should.

Vicky Featherstone

PAINES PLOUGH

The past few years have seen a massive explosion of new talent in British playwriting and Paines Plough is at the forefront of discovering, developing, producing and touring work by the best of these writers throughout the UK.

Formed in 1974, Paines Plough has maintained a consistent track record in discovering important new voices in British Theatre. It has been responsible for developing outstanding writers such as David Pownall, Stephen Jeffreys, Pam Gems, Tony Marchant, Christina Reid and, more recently, Michael Punter, Parv Bancil, Hilary Fannin, Stephen Greenhorn, Abi Morgan, Mark Ravenhill, Sarah Kane, Linda McLean and David Greig. Paines Plough is led by Vicky Featherstone, the company's fifth Artistic Director.

Recent Paines Plough productions include *The Cosmonaut's Last Message to the Woman he Once Loved in the Former Soviet Union* by David Greig, *Crave* by Sarah Kane, *Sleeping Around* by Hilary Fannin, Stephen Greenhorn, Abi Morgan and Mark Ravenhill, *Crazyhorse* by Parv Bancil and *The Wolves* by Michael Punter.

Paines Plough, funded by the Arts Council of England, produces two new plays a year and tours them throughout the UK. The company also runs TICKET TO WRITE, a totally unique nation-wide playwriting programme funded by the national lottery through the Arts Council of England. Our continual work with writers at every level of development is part of our core activity.

Writers are encouraged to be courageous in their work, to challenge our notions of theatre and the society we live in.

"the excellent Paines Plough" The Guardian '99

paines PLOUGH

Vicky Featherstone
Artistic Director

Belinda Hamilton
Administrative Director

Lucy Morrison
Marketing & Project
Co-ordinator TtW

Jessica Dromgoole
Literary Manager

Caroline Newall
Administrator

Chris O'Connell
Writer-in-Residence
(Supported by the Pearson Playwrights',
scheme sponsored by the Peggy Ramsey
Foundation)

paines PLOUGH
4th Floor
43 Aldwych
London WC2B 4DA

Tel. 0171 240 4533
Fax. 0171 240 4534
E-mail: paines.plough@dial.pipex.com

Lyric STUDIO Hammersmith

LYRIC
LINKS

The Lyric is a Registered Charity No 278518

RIDDANCE
TOUR DATES

10 August - 4 September
Traverse Theatre
Edinburgh Fringe Festival 1999

10 September
Cumbernauld Theatre

13 September
Guildhall Arts Centre
Grantham

15 September
Trinity Theatre and Arts Centre
Tunbridge Wells

20 September - 9 October
Lyric Theatre Hammersmith
London

13 - 14 October
Ustinov Studio
Bath Theatre Royal

18 - 19 October
Live Theatre
Newcastle

30 October
Theatre in the Mill
Bradford

1 November
Darlington Arts Centre

3 - 4 November
Leicester Haymarket Theatre

5 - 6 November
Stephen Joseph Theatre
Scarborough

9 - 10 November
Old Town Hall Arts Centre
Hemel Hampstead

12 - 13 November
Cambridge Drama Centre

RIDDANCE

Linda McLean

To Penny Gold,
Mark Ravenhill and Vicky Featherstone
with love and thanks

Kenny's flat.
There is a vacuum cleaner.
Kenny is in the middle of the room.
It looks as though he's waiting for something.
He is dressed for work.

KENNY: You are what you discard.
          That's a fact.
          In America there are people who specialise in
          reading what you throw away.
          Garbage graphologists they're called
          And they know something that you don't believe
          They know that the bits you throw away are
          In actual fact
          Your essence.

He turns his attention briefly to the vacuum cleaner and pats the handle.
His hand lingers.

          Everywhere you go
          You leave a trail
          Skin
          Hair
          Splutter
          Blood
          Piss
          And crap.
          Your litter is your DNA.
          True.
          It is.

          You need to take a look at that.
          Your droppings.
          Because
          Apart from some notable exceptions
          Hansel and Gretel being the ones who first spring
          to mind,

3

You don't want to leave a trail.
It's careless.

The advice of the garbage graphologist
Is
Don't put everything in one bin.
Separate
The bottles
And papers
Plastics
Cans books clothing electrical goods
And anything else which makes its way from
Your hands to
Your trash can
Bin
To you.

Think before you throw.

But
As for the more personal
Litter
Which they refer to
Strangely
As
Forensics
You don't have to watch every flake of skin as it
tumbles off and twirls to the ground.
It isn't necessary to become a martyr to detritus
I mean
You can
But
It's time consuming
And what would you do with it?

He gives the vacuum cleaner another pat.

There are ways of dealing with that.
Some are better than others.
More efficient.
This picks up everything.
Every

4

Single
Thing every cell
Will be in its safe-keeping
Until you decide
What you want to do with it.

There's safety in that.

Upstairs, unseen, a boy laughs.
Kenny looks up.
A woman says 'shoosh'.
Kenny waits.
Someone knocks at his door.
Kenny looks to the sound.
More knocking.
He still waits.
More knocking, this time it's a pattern of knocks that he
recognises.
He relaxes and goes to the door. (It has a lot of locking
mechanisms on it.)
By the time he opens it Clare, who has been knocking, is
irritated.

CLARE: What is it with you and that door?

She barges past him.

KENNY: Security. You know the knock.
CLARE: You're right, Kenny.
            I know the knock.
            And I know the theory behind the knock
            But every now and again
            I indulge myself
            With the hope that you'll let all that
            Go. (*She drops her bag.*)
KENNY: I would.
            You know I would
            If I could think of something else.
CLARE: Why don't you give me a key?
            (*She drops her coat.*)
KENNY: You're too careless.
CLARE: I'm not careless.

5

KENNY:	You lose things.
	Things that matter.
	Don't look at me like that.
	It's true.
	You've no hold on things.
	It's as if you don't care.
	But I do.
	I care what happens
	Especially in here.
	This is my place.
	And
	I don't mind people coming in.
	I like people to
	Warm the place up
	Make it homely
	But when they go
	It's mine again.
	I don't want anybody trampling over that.
CLARE:	I wouldn't trample.
KENNY:	You would trample more than anybody else
	Because you think you should.
	You think I should be messed up a bit.
	I know you.
	The shoes for instance.
CLARE:	I forgot.
KENNY:	I don't believe you forgot.
	Look at you.
	You didn't forget.
CLARE:	You kept me waiting.
KENNY:	And now you're sneering because you think something
	About the shoes.
	Howard Hughes.
	That's what you think.
CLARE:	Well.
KENNY:	Well?

Kenny waits. Clare takes off her shoes.

KENNY:	Thank you.
CLARE:	You worry me.
KENNY:	No I don't.
	You've known me since I was five.

6

	I might annoy you but I don't worry you.
CLARE:	I think you're getting worse.
KENNY:	I've always been like this, Clare.
CLARE:	Is that true?
KENNY:	I think so.
	I don't find myself any different.
	I don't like dangerous situations.
	I never have.
CLARE:	I know.
	I understand that.
	Somebody coming to you door to batter it down.

Kenny looks up at his ceiling.

	That's scary.
	But it isn't like that.
	Is it?
CLARE:	What?
	What is it?
KENNY:	Nothing.
CLARE:	What?
KENNY:	Na.
	It's nothing.
CLARE:	The point is Kenny.
	You knew it was me.
	You were expecting
	Me.
	That's not reasonable behaviour.
	Asking me to come over and then making me knock.
	I don't do that to you.
KENNY:	You look through your spyhole.
CLARE:	That's only sensible.
KENNY:	I've had bad luck with a spyhole.
CLARE:	Okay.
	I know your bad luck.
	You're right.
	Maybe you have always been like this.
	Maybe I'm expecting you to be different because you're older.
KENNY:	I don't know if that happens.
CLARE:	It does.

KENNY: Good.
            That'll be good then.

The boy upstairs runs across the floor.
Clare has a sudden thought.

KENNY: Did you hear that?
CLARE: Feet.
KENNY: Is that all?
CLARE: I had a dream this morning.
            No.
            A waking thing.
            About the boy.
KENNY: The boy.
CLARE: It was strange.
            He had a face.
            All the other times his face is blank
            But today
            He had a face.
            And I was so
            Pleased. I kept thinking
            The boy has got a face.
KENNY: Whose face has he got?
CLARE: What does that matter
            It had all the right bits.
            Eyes
            Nose
            Mouth.
            A proper face.
KENNY: Sit down.
CLARE: I'm okay.
            Honestly.
            It didn't upset me.
KENNY: No.
            This is why I had to speak to you.
            Listen.

Kenny plays his phone message.

FRANK'S VOICE:
            Dic Dic Tation
            Corpor Ation

How many buses
Are in the station?
Eh?
Fucking
Loads pal
And one's mine
Eh?
I'm at Victoria
And I'm starving
So
I'll get a bit of breakfast
And phone again.
Be in.

Kenny watches Clare.

KENNY:	See what I mean?
CLARE:	What?
	See what?
KENNY:	You.
	You're doing that premonition thing again.
CLARE:	What thing?
KENNY:	Your dream.
	Do you not get it?
	You dream about the boy and Frank phones.
CLARE:	Kenny
KENNY:	On the very same day.
CLARE:	Kenny, will you…(shut your face and listen)
KENNY:	Probably within a matter of hours.
CLARE:	*KENNY.*
	Listen to me.
	Frank knows nothing about the boy.
	Do you hear me?
KENNY:	Okay.
	I hear you.
	But you have to admit
	It's a very strong coincidence.
CLARE:	No.
	It could have been any day.
	I dream about him all the time.
KENNY:	Really?
	You never told me that.

CLARE:	Not all the time.
	Often.
KENNY:	I didn't know.
CLARE:	Why would I tell you?
KENNY:	I don't know.
	Only if it bothered you.
CLARE:	It doesn't bother me.
KENNY:	But this was the first time he had a face.
CLARE:	Yea.
KENNY:	Well then.
CLARE:	Okay.
	Yes, I said.

Kenny waits for her to say something else.

CLARE:	All right.
	It's a coincidence.
KENNY:	A strong coincidence.
	Frank hasn't phoned me in years.
	He hates the phone.
	But today
	He phones.
	And not only does he phone.
	He's here.
	At Victoria.
	He's coming over.
CLARE:	When did he phone?
KENNY:	About an hour ago.
	I phoned you straight away.
	What kept you?
CLARE:	I was watching a wee tot at the dump
	Climbing up the steps to the skip
	With the most
	Enormous
	Piece of cardboard
	Every step was/She could have fallen at any time
	I was scared to shut the office door
	In case it tipped the balance
	And her daddy was a good
	Two steps back.
	My heart was in my mouth.
KENNY:	Did she fall?

10

CLARE:	No.
	She was fine.
	Lovely wee thing.
KENNY:	I'm sure.
CLARE:	She just adored her daddy.
KENNY:	Clare.
	What are you going to do?
CLARE:	What are *you* going to do?
KENNY:	I don't know.
CLARE:	Me neither.

They think.

CLARE:	He doesn't know I'm here?
KENNY:	I don't think so.
	Who would tell him?
CLARE:	I don't know.
	Maybe *you've* been careless.
	Maybe you've said my name.
	I don't know.
KENNY:	I'm not careless.
	I haven't said your name to Frank.
CLARE:	Has *he*?
KENNY:	Has he what?
	Said *your* name?
CLARE:	*Has* he?

Kenny lets her know that he understands why she's asking.

CLARE:	Oh leave me alone.
KENNY:	Did you make a mistake?
CLARE:	Which one?
KENNY:	Leaving him.
	When he loved you.
	He did love you.
CLARE:	To the point of distraction.
	Kenny.
	And the distractions names were
	More than I can remember.
KENNY:	But he loved you the best.
	He was keeping you for last.
	Like the yolk on his egg.

CLARE:	And how long is that?
	Forty?
	Seventy?
	When is last Kenny?
	Hmm?
KENNY:	What if it's now?
	Eh?
	You and Frank?
CLARE:	No.
KENNY:	No?
CLARE:	He couldn't forgive me
	In a million years.
KENNY:	Are you sure?
CLARE:	I gave away his boy.
	I never told him
	There was a boy
	The chance of a boy
	Even
	Or a girl.
	I gave it away before it was born.
	When it was just a
	Thing
	That couldn't look me in the eye
	Or scream blue murder so that I'd want to shake
	it.
	Na.
	Me and Frank?
	It's out the question.
KENNY:	Okay.
	So you should be able to do this then.
CLARE:	Do what?
KENNY:	See him.
CLARE:	I didn't say I couldn't.
KENNY:	But you feel sick.
CLARE:	How do you know that?
KENNY:	Because *I* feel sick.
	And you feel like running.
CLARE:	But you're stuck.
KENNY:	So.
CLARE:	So.
KENNY:	What?
CLARE:	It's a simple matter of

	Control.
	You're good at that
KENNY:	You think we can control Frank?
CLARE:	You're looking at it the wrong way.
	Frank only does what we let him.
KENNY:	Are we talking about the same Frank?
CLARE:	I mean it.
	I can do it.
	I refuse to be scared of Frank.
	You think I'm scared.
	I'm not.
KENNY:	Who said anything about being scared?
CLARE:	You feel sick.
	You feel like running
	But you're stuck.
	What's that?
KENNY:	*I'm* not scared of him.
CLARE:	Of course you are.
	That's what that is.
KENNY:	I'm not scared he's going to hurt me.
	Jesus, Clare.
	When has he ever hurt me?
CLARE:	I don't know.
KENNY:	Never.
	He's like family.
	Like blood.
	If he hurt me he'd be hurting himself.
CLARE:	I don't know a fear that isn't about being hurt.
KENNY:	I do.
	I know a whole list of them.
CLARE:	Bloody Frank.
	He's the only thing that sticks out.
	Everything else fits
	But this
	This hiding from Frank
	It's weird.
	It makes my life feel weird.
	Maybe I should see him.
	Should I see him?
KENNY:	Will you tell him?
CLARE:	No.
	No.

I will not.
But
How will I not?
How will I look at his face
And not see the boy
And not say
The boy
And he'll know
He'll look at my face
And see something else
An old woman
An ugly old woman in Frank's eyes.
You won't tell him?

KENNY: You don't need to ask that.

CLARE: Good.

They wait for the phone to ring.

CLARE: Or.
You could come and stay with me
And we wouldn't
Have
To see him.
That's the choice
Is all I'm saying.
Giving you an
Option.

KENNY: I know.

CLARE: But you need to make up your mind.
Pretty swift.

KENNY: We should do what we want.

CLARE: We should do what's right.
Eh?

KENNY: Goes without saying.

The phone rings.
Neither of them pick it up.

FRANK: I'm still here
This is a fucking
Miserable place Kenny.
I'm starting to feel like

Like a dosser.
Know what I'm going to do?
I'm going to jump on a bus
Take a chance.
Eh?
Make my way to your place.
Worst comes to the worst
I can always kip on your landing.
Right?
See you then.
5p.
Nothing to say.
Fucking hate waste.
Aye
I have.
See your message?
Know what you sound like?
You sound like
Like
You sound like
I know who it is
It's the fucking insurance man.
No offence.

Beeeeeeep. The answering machine re-sets.

CLARE: Why is he coming now?
KENNY: I don't sound like the insurance man
            Do I?
CLARE: I mean.
            What is he going to do while he's here?
KENNY: I don't know.
            Drink.
            Liven the place up.
            You know what he's like.
CLARE: No.
            I haven't seen him since I was fifteen.
KENNY: He's Frank
            For God's sake.
            Frank's Frank.
CLARE: Is he?
KENNY: Well do I?

CLARE:	What?
KENNY:	Sound like the insurance man?
CLARE:	A bit.
KENNY:	No.
CLARE:	Yeah.
KENNY:	Which one?
CLARE:	Accidental damage and loss of limb.
KENNY:	No.
	He was horrible.
CLARE:	Sorry.
KENNY:	You sure you don't mean Life?
CLARE:	Life was sexy.
	My mother never went out when Life was coming round.
KENNY:	I do not sound like
	Accidental damage.
	Accidental damage had a lisp.
CLARE:	No.
	I'm just having you on.
KENNY:	I wonder who Frank means.
CLARE:	Frank.
	Yeah.
	He'll not be long in telling you.

They wait for the phone or the door.
Nothing.

KENNY:	What you said before
	About staying at your place.
	Is that still an option?
CLARE:	Is that what you want to do?
KENNY:	I don't know.
	I mean.
	How long *is* he going to be here?
	When people take a holiday
	They don't just take
	Two or three days.
	Do they?
	Chances are he's taken
	A week.
	And this is a busy week for me.
	I can't be going on the bevvy with Frank every night.

16

It might be easier to
Not be here. He's taking a big chance.
Turning up
Out the blue.
Just like that.
And expecting *me* to be here.
He could've let me know.
I could be on holiday.
What?
What?

CLARE: What if this is the right time?
KENNY: Is that a premonition?
CLARE: I don't get premonitions.
But
We've been keeping Frank out there for a long
time.
KENNY: I haven't been keeping him anywhere.
He's been keeping himself.
He knows where I am.
CLARE: Things have
Their own time.
KENNY: What?
What?
No.
No.
Things don't have time.
What are you talking about?
Things are where you put them.
This is what I mean about you.
You decide you're ready so you just
Let things go.
CLARE: Some things just fall.
KENNY: And you don't pay any mind to where they land.
Careless.
CLARE: Don't say that about me any more.
KENNY: I think it's true.
What's the face for?
Clare.
Hey.
What did I say that was so bad?
Lots of people are careless.
It's just the way they are.

17

CLARE:	You talk a lot of shite Kenny.
	And most of the time I put up with it because
	Because I love you.
	You're like my brother
	And I look out for you.
KENNY:	And I look out for you.
CLARE:	Yes
	You do.
	But I'm telling you now.
	One day you're going to speak
	One mouthful of shite too many
	And I'm going to
	Punch you one.
KENNY:	Clare.
CLARE:	I'm warning you.
KENNY:	Clare.
	You've been saying that for years.

Clare finds something about that funny.

CLARE:	So I have.
	Maybe I won't punch you then.
KENNY:	Maybe I'll punch you.
CLARE:	Is *that* a premonition?
KENNY:	I don't get premonitions.
	I wish I did.
	Everything always comes as a surprise to me.
	I hate it.

They've decided something.

CLARE:	Are you coming then?
KENNY:	It'll just be
	For a couple of days.
	Once he sees I'm not here he'll go home.
CLARE:	We should go now.
KENNY:	Definitely.

Clare gathers up her belongings.
Puts on her shoes.

| KENNY: | I think I'll bring the hoover. |

18

CLARE:	What for?
KENNY:	Just in case something happens to it.
	You never know.
	Is that a problem?
CLARE:	Bring it if you like.
KENNY:	Don't wait.
	Go and get the car.
	I'll switch everything off.
	Make it look as if I'm away.

Clare opens the door and looks out at the landing.

KENNY:	What is it?
CLARE:	Nothing.
KENNY:	What are you looking at?
CLARE:	Nothing.
	The landing.

She turns to Kenny so that he can see what she's thinking.
She steps on to the landing, closes the door and goes down the
stairs.

Upstairs the boy cries.
A man yells.
Kenny gets the vacuum cleaner.

KENNY: Under your bed there's the oose
                The soft fluffy stuff
                Different colours
                Bits of yourself
                Bits of jumpers
                Socks.
                Different bits
                From different days.
                Good bits
                Bad bits.

                Imagine
                That you could put all the good bits together
                And make a completely
                Good day
                Wouldn't you like that?
                Wouldn't that make you feel
                Optimistic?

                You can
                Watch this
                Filling up.
                Making a whole new week.
                See
                Here's the day you got up
                Went to work
                Sold ten hoovers
                Went out for dinner with Clare
                And came home to a quiet house.
                And down there
                With the silt
                Are the noises
                The sales you don't make
                The phone calls
                The dross.

The phone rings.
He ignores it.
He opens the door.
Frank is on the doorstep about to knock.

FRANK: Kenny Boy. (*The phone is still ringing.*)

Kenny loses his grip on the vacuum and one end drops.
Frank catches it.
He comes in.

KENNY: Frank.
FRANK: Get the phone.
            Get the phone.
KENNY: It's okay.
FRANK: No problem.
            I'll get the hoover.
KENNY: It's okay.
FRANK: I've got it.
KENNY: It's okay.
            The machine'll take care of it.

Frank and Kenny are both trying to manage the cleaner when
            Kenny's
mother speaks.

KENNY'S MOTHER
            Kenneth. This is your mother.
FRANK: It's your mother.
KENNY: I hear.
FRANK: I can manage the fucking hoover.
            Talk to you mother.
KENNY'S MOTHER:
            Kenneth. It's your mother here.
KENNY: I'll phone her back later.
FRANK: It's your fucking mother.
KENNY'S MOTHER:
            Okay son. Some other time.

The phone message ends.
Frank lets go the vacuum cleaner.

FRANK:	That was your mother.
KENNY:	I know it was my mother. (*Kenny picks up the vacuum and places it carefully against a wall.*).
FRANK:	Your fucking mother phones Kenny You don't let the fucking Machine talk to her.
KENNY:	She doesn't mind. I had my hands full.
FRANK:	Wouldn't let go you mean. Hanging on to the hoover like it was The thing.
KENNY:	I was on my way out.
FRANK:	So I see.
KENNY:	I was late.
FRANK:	Big fucking hurry.
KENNY:	You're lucky you caught me in.
FRANK:	Aye.
KENNY:	Aye.
FRANK:	You knew I was coming.
KENNY:	I did.
FRANK:	Aye.
KENNY:	Aye yourself.
FRANK:	Were you running away, Kenny?
KENNY:	I wasn't running.
FRANK:	Of course you were. You're always running away from Something. That's all right. I know you. I said to your mother Don't phone and tell him your news Margaret/
KENNY:	Margaret? You call my mother Margaret?
FRANK:	I'm your mother's best pal. Don't phone him Margaret I said Because he'll just run.
KENNY:	What news?
FRANK:	I should've listened to my self. I knew When I phoned from Victoria It was a mistake.

KENNY: What news?
            What news?
FRANK: Your mother's sick.

Kenny waits to see what he thinks about this.

KENNY: No she isn't.
FRANK: She fucking is.
KENNY: She's fine.
            You just heard her.
            She sounds fine.
FRANK: I'm telling you.
            She's sick.
KENNY: She is not sick.
            She is not.
            She
            How sick?
FRANK: Bad.
KENNY: She can't be bad.
            She would've told me.
FRANK: Over the phone?
KENNY: She would've told me.
FRANK: On your fucking screening machine?
            Oh aye.
            'Hello Kenneth. This is your mother here. I'm
            dying. Beeep.'
KENNY: Dying?
FRANK: No.
            Maybe.
            I don't know.
            I never meant to say it like that.
            You.
            Fuck.
            She's getting chemotherapy.
KENNY: Chemotherapy.
            That doesn't mean she's dying.
FRANK: It means she's sick but
            Doesn't it?
KENNY: But not dying.
            The way you said it.
            Are you trying to scare me?
            Chemotherapy.

	That's not dying any more.
	Everybody gets chemotherapy.
	They give it to cats and dogs for Gods sake.
FRANK:	You need to come home.
KENNY:	No can do.
FRANK:	What?
KENNY:	I can't.
FRANK:	You will.
KENNY:	Of course I will.
	I mean
	I am going to.
	I just can't go right at this minute.
FRANK:	Tomorrow.
KENNY:	Next week.
FRANK:	First
	Thing
	Tomorrow
	Morning.
KENNY:	It'll need to be next week.
FRANK:	No.
KENNY:	It's work.
	I can't get out of it.
FRANK:	Of course you can.
	It's the one time you can.
KENNY:	I can't.

The woman's footsteps go upstairs.

FRANK:	Kenny
	If I need to stoat you off the wall till you're
	senseless and
	Drag you back
	That's how we'll go.

Upstairs the boy tumbles his whelkies.
The man yells at him.
Kenny pretends he doesn't hear anything.
Frank waits.
It stops.

FRANK:	What the fuck is that?
KENNY:	What?
FRANK:	Mr Noisy up the stair?

24

KENNY:	Is that what that is?
FRANK:	Did you not hear what I heard?
KENNY:	No.
FRANK:	What do you mean no?
	How do you know what I heard?
KENNY:	Because you're getting edgy
	And I don't know that there's anything to get edgy
	about.
FRANK:	Is that right?
	Who's up there?
KENNY:	I don't know.
FRANK:	Of course you know.
KENNY:	Some guy.
	Some woman.
FRANK:	Does he lift his hands to her?
KENNY:	I don't know.
	Maybe.
FRANK:	Anybody else?
KENNY:	I don't know.
FRANK:	One?
	Two?
KENNY:	Just the one
	I think.

Frank waits for Kenny to tell him the rest.
Kenny footers.

KENNY:	I think it's a boy.
FRANK:	Fuck.
KENNY:	I'm going to move.
	They just moved in.
	I'm moving.
	I am.
	It used to be nice here.
	I don't know what happened.
	Used to be two old biddies lived up there.
	Never made a sound.
	They baked.
	Every weekend.
	They baked bread for the whole week.
	As soon as you stepped into the close you could
	smell the bread.

It was magic.

I don't know what happened.

I don't even know if they died.

Whole close smells of pish.

Stale beer and pish.

I hate it.

FRANK: Has he been to the door?

KENNY: No.

FRANK: Because

If he bothers you.

KENNY: I've never even seen him.

FRANK: But if he does.

I'm just saying.

You know.

KENNY: I don't even know if he's

Real.

FRANK: What?

KENNY: I wasn't sure.

Sometimes you hear things

You know.

Innocent things

But you hear them as if they're

Not innocent.

And then you realise they were nothing.

Nothing at all

And that makes you wonder

If you're hearing anything right.

Sometimes I wonder if I'm hearing the same

things as everybody else.

Do you never wonder that?

FRANK: Aye.

KENNY: You wonder?

FRANK: You hear what you hear.

You can't hear what everybody else hears.

They're all hearing their own stuff anyway.

Very few people hear just what there is and

nothing more. Very few.

In fact

I'm only saying that on the off chance that they

exist.

I've never met anybody like that.

KENNY: Yes you have.

FRANK:	No I fucking haven't.
KENNY:	No.
	I mean
	I have.
FRANK:	Oh yeah?
KENNY:	And not only does she
	Hear
	What there is, she
	Sees
	What there is as well
	She doesn't spend her life wishing it was different.
FRANK:	And who is this
	Hear all
	See all
	Woman?
KENNY:	Who?
FRANK:	Her name.
KENNY:	None of your business.
FRANK:	Funny name.
	Funny thing to say
	A hiding thing
	Hiding what?
	More than a name
	I bet you.
	Eh?
KENNY:	Look.
	Your interest
	Begins and ends
	With her ability to hear things
	Just the way they are.
	And I'm telling you
	She does.
FRANK:	Na.
KENNY:	What do you mean 'Na'?
FRANK:	I mean Na.
	I meet people.
	You know me.
	In my line of work I meet a lot of people.
	I've never seen it.
KENNY:	Don't take this the wrong way, Frank
	But working in The Centurion bar is hardly what
	you'd call

	Cosmopolitan.
	Is it? I mean.
	You couldn't say you meet a
	Genuine
	Cross section of society.
	Now could you?
FRANK:	I meet your mother.
	I take your mother to the
	Fucking shops because she's
	Not well enough
	To take the bus.
	Cheeky cunt.
	You're a cheeky cunt, Kenny.
KENNY:	Right.
FRANK:	You are
	One
	Cheeky
	Cunt.
KENNY:	Cunt yourself.

Now they're pleased to see each other.

FRANK:	Hey.
KENNY:	Hey.
FRANK:	Cunt.

Kenny finds something about that funny.

KENNY:	You're looking good, Frank.
FRANK:	I know.
	I'm peaking.
KENNY:	Peaking?
FRANK:	Getting as good as I'm going to get.
	Look at me.
	Just spent the whole night
	On the bus
	With my head
	Fucking
	Rattling against a window
	And I still look good eh?
	Imagine how I'm going to look after a night's kip
	Eh?

28

	I needed to see your face Kenny.
KENNY:	You nearly missed me.
	Five more minutes and I was out of here.
FRANK:	Time is on my side then.
KENNY:	What?
FRANK:	Time is on my side.
KENNY:	No.
	No.
	Time doesn't take sides.
	It's incidental.
FRANK:	No
	No Kenny
	Because
	When time is on your side
	It's the very best of company.
	It's like
	A benediction.
	You catch the bus.
	Even though it should have left.
	The driver's an old mate who owes you a favour
	Which is handy
	When the finances are low.
	You catch your pal
	On his way out the door.
	What else?
	Who knows what else
	Will go right
	When time's on your side?

Clare comes back to Kenny's mind..

FRANK:	Eh?
	Kenny?
KENNY:	Aye.
	Who knows?
FRANK:	I get the feeling *you* know.
KENNY:	Know what?
FRANK:	Something.
	Something there
	Kenny.
	In your face.
	I know that face.

What is it?
Eh?
Eh?
You're worrying me now.
Kenny.
What's going on?
Pal.
What?

Clare knocks on the door.
Kenny recognises it and looks to the door.
Frank connects the two things.

FRANK: I know that.

Clare knocks the knock again.

FRANK: That
            Stupid
            Fucking
            Knock.
            You're not still doing that
            Are you?
KENNY: Frank.
            I know who that is.
FRANK: Of course you do.
KENNY: Aye.
            I know.
            But so do you.
FRANK: *I* know who it is?
            How do I know who it is?

Clare knocks again.
It's a bad tempered knock.

FRANK: The only other person
            Apart from you and me
            Who knew that knock
            Was
KENNY: Clare.

Kenny opens the door.

30

Clare comes in.
From upstairs comes the faint sound of the woman singing
Summertime
while she rocks.

FRANK: Am I drowning, or what?
                Are you real?
                Are you?
CLARE: As real as you.
FRANK: I've been seeing you for years
                And it's never been you.
CLARE: I haven't been seeing you.(*Summertime is barely*
                audible.)
FRANK: No.
                Why would you?
                You've known where I am.
                You could come and find me
                Any time.
                You only see the people who leave you.
CLARE: I thought it was the dead.(*Summertime goes.*)
                You only see the dead.
FRANK: No.
CLARE: That's good.
                I'm glad.
                Because that worried me.

Frank notices Kenny.

FRANK: This is
                Her?
                She's been here?
                All this time?
KENNY: No.
                Not all the time.
                Ten years.
                She was somewhere else before that.
FRANK: Ten years?
KENNY: I didn't know you were looking for her.
                You never said.
FRANK: I never said?
                You mean you never knew?
                You never noticed my torn face?

FRANK:	(*to Clare*) *You* knew.
	You knew I'd be looking.
CLARE:	No.
FRANK:	Fucking did.
	Fucking.
	Fucking hiding out.
	Fuck.
	No.
	No.
	I know what I mean.
	I know how to say what I mean.
	You think I'm some
	Some wordless bastard.
	I'm not.
	I can gather them.
	Gather them and say what I mean.
	You've been hiding out.
	Yes you have
	Because if you weren't
	If that wasn't true
	He would've told me you were here.
	You would've told me you were here.
	And you never.
	And *he* never.
	You told him not to.
	Didn't you?
	Didn't you?
KENNY:	She never.
CLARE:	Kenny.
KENNY:	What?
CLARE:	Yes.
	I told him.

Upstairs a door bangs.
And then another.

KENNY:	Careless.
	Careless.
CLARE:	No.
	(*to Frank*) I told him not to tell you I was here.
FRANK:	And so he never.
KENNY:	There you go.

32

	Dropping everything.
	You don't look.
	You don't care what happens.
CLARE:	Kenny thinks I'm careless, Frank.
	He doesn't believe in a right time
	Or place.
	He thinks that days only happen
	Once.
	And people never go back.
	He doesn't know that we're all magnets for each other.
FRANK:	Fucking magnets.
	That's right.
KENNY:	That's pish.
	Now.
	I mean it.
	Chuck it.
	You two.
	Talking like that.
	Just.
	Watch it now.
CLARE:	We're worrying him.
FRANK:	No.
KENNY:	Yes.
	Yes you are.
	Things happen you know.
	You start talking like that and things happen.
	And then they're never the same.
CLARE:	Never the same.
FRANK:	Never.

Clare sees something in Frank's face that makes her turn sharply.

FRANK:	What is it?
CLARE:	Nothing.
FRANK:	(*to Clare*) You turned.
	You saw her Kenny
	Didn't you?
KENNY:	It was something in your face, Frank.
FRANK:	Something in my face?
KENNY:	Maybe you remind her of somebody.

CLARE:	(*to Kenny*) What are you doing?
KENNY:	I'm saying.
	This is what happens when you're careless
	Clare.
FRANK:	Is there something wrong with my face?
	Eh?
CLARE:	No.
FRANK:	What?
CLARE:	No.
	Nothing.
FRANK:	What is it then?
	Kenny?
	What?
	Clare.
	What in my face?
CLARE:	Nothing.
FRANK:	Something.
CLARE:	Okay.
	You used to look different.
FRANK:	No I never.
	Not really.
	I mean
	A few minor adjustments with time
	But pretty much the same old mug
	Eh?
	Eh?
CLARE:	You never used to look like
	Your father.

All three really see each other and remember.

KENNY:	You don't look like your father Frank.
	She's just saying that.
	Aren't you, Clare?
	You're just saying that to cover what you really
	think.
CLARE:	He does.
FRANK:	No.
	That's okay.
	He was a big drunk that liked hurting people.
	Fucking big miserable bastard.
	It's okay.

But I don't really think I look like him.
For a start
His eyes rolled
And his mouth hung open.
Everything just
Spilling right out of it

Kenny shuts his eyes.

Spit
Blood
His tongue
Everything.
It made you boke just to look at him.
His nose
Frothing.
Purple.
Couldn't speak a word.
Kenny?

Kenny opens his eyes.

No.
Even drunk
I don't think you could say I look
Anything like him.
CLARE: Before.
I meant before he
KENNY: fell.
Before he fell.
See.
You see what happens.
See what you've done.
See?
Frank
I don't get premonitions.
Ask anybody.
But I could have told you this was going to
happen.
You think you can just barge into people's lives.
Unannounced.
And it'll all be okay.

But look.
Look what happens.
We're not the kind of people that can just
Pick up
After twenty years
And go for a pint and be happy.
Are we?
We're not.
We can't do it.
So (*to Frank*)
Why don't you stay where you stay.
(*to Clare*) You stay where you stay.
And I'll stay (*He considers upstairs.*)
Where I stay.
And that's how we'll manage it.
That's how it works.

FRANK: I can go for a pint.
KENNY: You can go for ten pints.
I've never seen you go for one.
FRANK: I can go for a pint.
A couple of pints well.
KENNY: *She* can't.
CLARE: She?
KENNY: You.
You can't go for a pint.
You've got a tendency to
Lose your grip on things
As it is.
CLARE: I can go for a pint.
KENNY: You think so?
CLARE: I can go for a pint.
FRANK: Fuck's sake, Kenny.
We can go for a fucking pint.
Things are not that bad.
(*to Clare.*) We can.
Eh?
No?
What do you say?
CLARE: Of course.
Of course I can.
Kenny?
KENNY: What?

CLARE:	Is there something you want to say?
	Something you need to get off your chest?
FRANK:	What are you talking about?
KENNY:	Time in between Frank.
	Twenty years.
	A lot happens.
	You haven't been filled in.
	But no.
	There's nothing.
	I've nothing to say.
	For now.
CLARE:	Good.
	I'm glad.
KENNY:	You think you can go for a pint.
	That's fine by me.
	You can just
	Operate
	Up there
	On that blah blah level
	Great.
	No danger of you
	Two pints down the road
	Forgetting to forget.
CLARE:	No danger.
KENNY:	That's fine then.
CLARE:	It is.
FRANK:	You two.
	I forgot you were a pair of weirdo's.
KENNY:	Aye.
	That's right Frank.
	And you're normal.

Frank finds something about that funny.

FRANK:	Ah come on.
	First pint's mine.
KENNY:	I thought you were skint.
FRANK:	I've always got the price of a pint.
	Not to mention the bus money I never spent.
	And
	It's a bit of a celebration, isn't it?
	Eh?

The three of us.
Eh?

No-one makes a move.

FRANK:	Maybe not.
KENNY:	Right enough.
CLARE:	Na.
	Anyway
	It's pissing out there.
FRANK:	And who needs that?
	Eh?
	Fucking
	More rain.
KENNY:	Not me.
FRANK:	Not anybody.
CLARE:	Maybe the Africans.
FRANK:	Aye well.
	Put it in a bag and send it to them.

Each of them is waiting for something.
Nothing materialises.

KENNY:	How far is Africa?
CLARE:	Far.
FRANK:	Too far to go in a bus.
KENNY:	But
	How far?
FRANK:	I'd still find you.

Kenny suddenly hates Frank.

KENNY:	Sometimes I dream you're dead.
FRANK:	Sometimes I nearly am.
	Maybe it's not a dream
	Maybe it's a premonition.
CLARE:	Kenny doesn't get/(premonitions).
FRANK:	Sure he does.
	When you've as many fears as Kenny
	Some of them are bound to come true.
	And you know what Kenny's worst fear is
	Don't you?

CLARE:	Yes.
FRANK:	You do?
CLARE:	I don't know.
	Maybe.
FRANK:	No maybes.
	Kenny's worst fear
	Is
	That I'm going to take him home
	Make him walk
	In the close
	Up the stairs
	Over the landing
	And leave him there.
	That's it.
	Being left
	On his own
	On that landing.
CLARE:	It's a scary place.
	That landing
	I wouldn't like to be left there.
FRANK:	You wouldn't go to
	Fucking Africa
	To get away from it but
	Would you?
CLARE:	It's not what I'm scared of.
FRANK:	I know what you're scared of.
KENNY:	He doesn't know.
	You don't Frank.
	Honest.
FRANK:	Whisper whisper
	We know
	You don't
	Living here
	In this fucking
	Cocoon. You
	You are the people
	Who know
	Nothing.
	I know.

Upstairs the boy whispers.

FRANK:	Aye.
	I do.
	You're scared that it's all going to
	Pass you by
	Aren't you?
	You women
	You/
CLARE:	What?
FRANK:	Women.
	You
	Woman.
	Your age.
	No weans.
	It's scary.
	It's all right for me.
	All right for Kenny.
	But you women
	Different story.
	And I know how old you are Clare.
CLARE:	Oh aye
	Biological clocks
	They're terrifying
	Right enough.
FRANK:	Away you go
	You're a born mother
	If ever I met one.

That wipes the smile right off her face.

	Look at how you mother Kenny.
	Eh?
	You trying to tell me
	You haven't been hearing the patter of tiny feet?
	I don't believe it for a minute.
	Only thing that puzzles me
	Is
	How come you've none?
	Eh?
CLARE:	You don't know that.
FRANK:	Right enough.
	Maybe you have.
	Twenty years.

40

Maybe you've ten.
But I don't see it
In your face.
And I'm looking at faces.
Fathers faces
And they've all
Two
Three
Lines under their eyes.
Dead tired
Paying attention
But
Dead tired all the same.
You
Look at you
You haven't got ten.
You haven't got any.
That's you and me
In the same boat.

CLARE: We're not.

FRANK: How do you know?
How do you know
That what's happened to you
Hasn't happened to me?
That time in between?
That
Fucking
Enormous
Time
You walk in that door
And it's gone
There's
One minute Then
Next minute Now.

KENNY: No.
No.
We're older
We're different.
We've lived
A different life
Right Clare?
That's right.

	I don't even feel as if
	It was me.
	I mean/
CLARE:	A minute Kenny.
KENNY:	You can't be held/ (responsible)
CLARE:	I said
	A minute here.
	You're butting in.
	And Frank was talking to me
	Am I right Frank?
	That was me you were talking to there?
FRANK:	I was just saying
CLARE:	How you were wondering
	Why I had no weans.
	Right?
FRANK:	Well
	Nice looking woman like yourself
	You can't be short of offers.
CLARE:	I'm not.
FRANK:	See
	So
	We're agreeing then.
CLARE:	No.
	Yes.
	I don't know. What I mean is
	I have an opportunity here
	A right time
	Has presented itself
	Out of pleasant moment.
	The chance to do something
	Not in anger
	I'm reluctant to let it go.
FRANK:	Why would you?
	There's nothing you could say
	That would change me
	How I feel
CLARE:	And I do mind
	How you feel.
FRANK:	I know that.
CLARE:	And you're right.
	Your vision of me
	Is dear.

	I see that.
	That explains a lot to me.
KENNY:	You're not being fair.
	You have to think of
	All of us.
	You don't know
	You can only imagine
	What'll happen.
CLARE:	It's not often
	Is it
	That you really have choice?
	Not that you know of
	Eh?

It's only when you
Don't know what to do
That you think about choice
Which is a pig
Isn't it?
Because
That's the time you're least able
To make one.
You think I'm oblique
I'm not
I'm playing for time
I don't know what to do
Because on the one hand
There's right
And on the other
There's
I don't know what
And I should definitely go for right
Goes without saying
But I have
The sneaking suspicion
That right could be
Wrong
And I'm aware that having said so much
I'm more than half way there
All you have to do
Is ask
The right question
Because I am

	I am
	Undecided.
KENNY:	She had a dream.
CLARE:	It's not that.
KENNY:	She had a dream
	And now she thinks
	It means something
	She's/It's coincidence
	And
	A dream for Christ's sake
	It's no excuse for /(ruining a life)
FRANK:	I know about a dream.
KENNY:	What?
CLARE:	Which dream?
FRANK:	My dream
	Jesus
	Who else's.
	You think I know your dream?
CLARE:	I don't know.
	What *was* your dream?
FRANK:	Sand
CLARE:	Oh.
KENNY:	See.
	Sand.
FRANK:	And it was
	Kind-of me
	But it wasn't
	You know?
CLARE:	yeah
KENNY:	yeah
FRANK:	I was burying my Da in the sand
	Couldn't get enough sand to cover his chest
	So I'm digging
	And pouring
	And I don't notice that it's actually me
	In the sand now
	Not my Da
	Till I finally cover the last chest hair
	And in my dream
	Maybe this was real
	Because it woke me up
	Me

44

Pulling a hair on my chest
And I woke up thinking
Well if that's me under the sand
Who the fuck is that
Trying to bury me then
And as soon as I thought it
I knew.
Because it's nobody
There's nobody there
Burying me in the sand
And
The thing is
I'd like that.
There's a shock for you.
Eh?
See your faces.
No
I mean it
I've reached a point
Where I'm ready to start
Being
Real.
Slow learner, I know.
And everybody else started a long time ago.
So
Not much choice.
You might say
In the women.
Because I don't want somebody that's already got
one.
A boy.
A son.
That's my dream.
A boy
To bury me in the sand
And it's a good one
Eh? Because
Because I never expected to have it.
You're surprised.
It surprises me.
I thought
Not that I really thought about it

Not really
I mean.
Only in the way that everybody does
Weans
You know
But then
When I did think
I thought that I could just about handle a wee
lassie.
No reminders.
A fresh start.
And I can see myself
Holding one.
Giving her a cuddle.
I'm sure I could.
I can see it
But my heart
My heart
Is set on a boy.
Did you think I'd ever want a boy?
Eh?
Clare?
Did you ever think that?

CLARE: No.
I never did.

FRANK: There you are then.
Me neither.
But look now.
Eh?
And that's what gets me.
About you Kenny.
I'm sorry Clare
You say question
And the thing that comes to mind
Is not you
It's Kenny

KENNY: Forget me.
Do her.

FRANK: No
I can't
It's a layer thing.
And I can't see past it

	Because it bothers me
	And it's got build-up
	You know
	I can actually feel my neck stiffening
	And my shoulders.
	Like some cunt's wound me up.
	So I definitely think
	This is the one I need to ask.
	(*to Kenny*) Do you not love your mother?
KENNY:	I don't see how you get from sand
	To me loving my mother.
FRANK:	Do you?
	Do you?
KENNY:	I don't know.
FRANK:	You don't know?
KENNY:	No.
	I really don't.
	She used to cuddle me
	And ask 'Do you love your Mammy?'
	And I'd say 'Yes, I do love you Mammy'
	But I only said it
	Because I knew it was the right answer
	I didn't know it
	How could I?
	I'll only know
	When she dies
	She's always said that
	'You'll only appreciate me when I'm gone'
	I think she's right.
FRANK:	So
	What.
	You're going to wait till she dies
	To discover that you love her
	And then be sorry?
	Does the fact that she's
	Sick
	Not count?
CLARE:	Your mother's sick, Kenny?
FRANK:	She's getting chemotherapy.
KENNY:	See.
	Chemotherapy.
CLARE:	That's … (serious stuff.)

	I mean.
	That's cancer.
	Right?
KENNY:	Cancer.
	Jesus.
	You know.
	Cancer.
	And guide dogs.

                    I mean.
                    That's cancer.
                    Right?
KENNY: Cancer.
                    Jesus.
                    You know.
                    Cancer.
                    And guide dogs.
                    Have you any idea how much money they get?
                    There are more guide dogs than there are blind
                    people.
                    Did you know that?
                    And seventy Eighty NINEty per cent even
                    Of cancers
                    Are completely curable.
                    So.
                    You know.
                    It's not the end of the world. I mean.
                    Jeez oh
                    It's spastics I feel sorry for.
                    Whatever you want to call them.
                    Who gives *them* money?
                    Nobody.
                    If there's one thing I wouldn't want to be in this
                    world
                    It's a spastic.
CLARE: Kenny.
                    It's okay.
                    It's going to be okay.
KENNY: No.
                    No it isn't okay.
                    I'm not okay.
                    You.
                    It's okay for you.
                    You can turn up at your work any time you like.
                    Me?
                    I've got appointments.
                    There are people out there with dirty houses
                    Waiting for things to get cleaner.
                    Waiting for me.
                    If I say I'm going to be at a place
                    I've got to be there.

Or else.
And I've got to be there now.
So.

Kenny picks up the hoover.

KENNY: And you can take that look off your face.
            Faces.
            Because you know nothing.
            Nothing.
FRANK: Where are you going with that?
KENNY: I don't know.

Frank takes the hoover.

FRANK: You're going nowhere.
            You're going to sit down on your arse and phone
            your mother.
            Pick it up
            And tell her you're coming home.
KENNY: I won't.
FRANK: I would've said
            Before this
            That I couldn't imagine you doing
            Anything
            That would change my
            Deep down good opinion of you
            But this does.
            A punch on the mouth
            Is what this deserves.
            See.
            Without being maudlin -
            Because I haven't even had a pint
            So maudlin's not in the equation -
            But
            And you might find this hard to believe
            But
            The thing I keep thinking
            About my Da
            And how he died
            And all that
            The thing that really gets me

49

Is
I never had the time -
You know
Now that I'm a bit wiser
Well
Older
And I know the difference between being a
bastard
And being a
Prisoner.   See
I never got the chance to say that.
I never got the chance to see if there was
Any single bit
Of him
I liked.

CLARE: Your Da was/
FRANK: I know what he was
I know what he was to me
To my Ma
But I don't know what he used to be.

KENNY: He hammered the living daylights out of you.
FRANK: Aye
But when he was four.
What was he
When he was four?

KENNY: Hammering the living daylights out of two year
olds.

FRANK: Is that right?
You know that
Do you?
Eh?
Or is that your idea of a joke?
Eh??

KENNY: Sorry.
FRANK: My Da The Drunk
Used to say
Watch the jokers, son
They're hiding something.
And look at you
Eh?
Look what you were hiding.

CLARE: I did my own hiding.

FRANK:	Aye
	A right wee Russian doll
	Hiding under the hiding
	Don't know what I think about that yet.
	I'm fast losing patience with Kenneth here
	But you're a different kettle of fish
	Allthegether.
	I don't know what I'm losing with you.
CLARE:	You don't.
FRANK:	I have the feeling you know.
	Eh?
	Magnets you said.
KENNY:	No.
	No.
	Magnets.
	See
	You find magnets in rocks.
	Rocks, Frank.
	Not people.
	In people it's hormones.
FRANK:	Says you.
	Here's what I say.
	I'm on my own.
	She's on her own.
CLARE:	She?
FRANK:	You.
	You still like me.
	Look at yourself.
	Eh?
	I know when I'm being liked.
	And I've always wanted you.
	From day one.
	You know that.
	You just have to put your hand out and I'm there.
	You can see that.
KENNY:	She's here Frank.
	That's all.
	It's a coincidence.
	Don't go painting yourself a picture.
FRANK:	What do you think of my picture Clare?
CLARE:	Think?
	As if thinking had anything to do with me and you.

51

	You and me.
	We were/
KENNY:	Bad for each other.
FRANK:	No.
CLARE:	No.
FRANK:	See.
CLARE:	*He* was bad for me.
	(*to Frank*) You were bad for me.
FRANK:	No.
KENNY:	(*to Frank*) You were bad for me as well.
FRANK:	I was good.
CLARE:	You were a headcase
	Frank
	When you weren't pished and fighting
	You were pished and fucking somebody
	Up a close.
FRANK:	She's bitter about that.
	Is that a good sign?
	Kenny.
	What do you think?
KENNY:	No.
FRANK:	No?
	I'm not so sure.
	Definitely something still going on there.
CLARE:	You think you know something.
	Fine
	You think you see something
	Well good
	Keep looking
	But don't
	For a minute
	Imagine
	That you know me.
FRANK:	It's not my fault.
	This is my time of life.
	Might even be my place.
	You call it coincidence.
	But here's what I know.
	It doesn't matter what you want
	Either of you
	Because the way things are looking
	The way they smell

```
              Tells me
              That it's my time.
              What I want
              Is the thing.
              And I do know
              What I want.
KENNY:        That's good.
              That's great.
              You know what you want.
              I know what I want.
```

Heavy footsteps go up the close stairs.
The boy whimpers.

```
KENNY:    I want you to go away from me.
          This was never meant to be my life.
          There was a whole
          Other life
          Mapped out for me.
          And but for you
          But for your Da
          I'd be having that life
          You've embroiled me.
          Clogged up my life with all your
          Rubbish
CLARE:    You're not being fair.
KENNY:    And you.
          You're as bad as he is.
          I can hardly breathe
          For the/Smell you say.
          You're right.
          I can smell it.
          Look at you
          The two of you
          This is my home
          Do you understand that?
          My home
          And you're in here
          Messing it up
          Trampling all over the place
          Crapping
          All over me.
```

	You two thegether?
	It's meant
	Definitely
	Because
	You're a midden
	The pair of you.
FRANK:	Will I hit him?
CLARE:	He doesn't know what he's saying.
FRANK:	But I want to.
	I do.
	I think I've wanted to hit you
	For a
	Very
	Long
	Time, Kenny Boy.
	Never realised it till now
	More than that
	I feel a happiness
	At the thought of you being hurt.
	A thrill even
	Like a first drink
	Good in itself
	But even better with the prospect of more to come.
	I could hurt you Kenny.
	I never knew that.

Phone rings.

FRANK: Pick it up.

Frank closes in.
Kenny doesn't move.
Frank draws back his head slightly.
Kenny doesn't move.

FRANK: Pick it up.
           You know who it is.
           Pick it up.

Kenny doesn't pick it up.
There's no message.
Frank draws his upper body back, ready to stick the head on
Kenny.

CLARE: Frank.
            Frank.
            Okay Frank.
            Be your Da.
            Go on.
            Hurt him.
            He deserves it.
            Eh?
            He took you in Frank.
            He saved your life how many times?
            Hit him hard then.
            Go on.
            Go on.

Frank backs off.
Half of him can't believe what he's doing.
The other half wants to keep on going.

FRANK: There's a
            Lie
            Locked up in me, Clare.
CLARE: In me too.
FRANK: Aye
            But I don't know what it is.
            With most people
            They know their own lies
            I don't.
            And it's fierce.
            I sometimes think it's going to
            Eat me alive.
            I want to see it
            Look it in the eye
            But I can't
            I only know what it feels like.
            Kenny.
            Kenny.
            You need to talk your mother.
            Don't make me want to kill you.
            She needs looking after.
            You're all she's got
            All she's ever had.
            I can't do it.

55

I can't.
My Ma had brown hair.
It wasn't very nice.
It was frizzy
But it was brown
Once
Once
She had a whole face.
Not that
Skull they get
And your mother's starting to look
Like my Ma.
And I never wanted to look after my Ma
In the first place
But who else was there?
Nobody.
But here are you.
You have to/I can't do it for you.
You can't leave a woman with a skull for a face
To fend for herself.
Can you?
Can you?

From upstairs comes the knock.

KENNY: He knows the knock.
CLARE: Who?
KENNY: Mr Noisy Up The Stair.
CLARE: I didn't know you had a Mr Noisy Up The Stair.
           You never told me that.
KENNY: Why would I?
CLARE: Only if it bothered you.
           Kenny.
KENNY: I'm moving.
           I'm moving.
           Shite.
           I need a new knock now.
           Don't I?
           If he knows the knock
           How do I know who it is at the door?

The boy knocks the knock again.

FRANK:	What if it's not him?
	What if it's the boy?
CLARE:	There's a boy?
FRANK:	Up the stair.
CLARE:	How do you know?
FRANK:	I heard him.
CLARE:	Have you seen him?
FRANK:	No.
CLARE:	How do you know it's a boy?
FRANK:	He cries like a boy.
CLARE:	He cries?
	Kenny?
KENNY:	What?
	WHAT?
CLARE:	A crying boy?
	And you never told me?

Third louder knocking.

KENNY:	Everywhere I go
	There's a crying boy.
	And him
	Him up the stairs.
	(*to Frank*) And you.
	That's what I hear.
	Your Da
	Thumping you
	And you
	Whimpering.
	And it's like it's me.
	Like it's happening to me.
	And he gets you.
	He gets you and he leathers you.
	Up and down the stairs.
	I hear you running.
	Running to get away.
	But he gets you in a corner
	And you scream
	So I put my hands over my ears.
	And I hum.
	So I won't hear it.
	Or I hoover.

FRANK:	But Kenny
	This is me here.
KENNY:	And I've done my best
	To keep myself
	Safe.
	Safety and security.
	First principles.
	Right?
	You think it's funny
	But things need to be kept in place.
	Otherwise they get
	Completely
	Out of control
	And before you know where you are
	You're back living that life
	In the same place
	With the same faces
	And it's all been for nothing.
	And you start to get/I'm getting
	Beyond belief
	And shrinking. I've seen myself curled up in ball
	The size of an elephant
	Squeezed into a wee room
	But now
	Now
	I'm the mouse
	And the room's the elephant.
FRANK:	Is he sick?
CLARE:	He's not sick.
	He's just
	Anxious.
FRANK:	Hey
	Kenny Boy
	Come on
	I'll not hurt you
	I was just being
	The thing
	You know
	The thing to
	Wisen you up.
	Keep you right.
	Eh?

Don't go funny on me.
Eh Pal?

Kenny waits for something.
He looks upstairs.
Nothing.
Frank makes a move towards him.
Kenny waves him away.

KENNY: Me
            Go funny on you?
            That's good.
            All I did
            All I ever did
            Was live under you
            That was it.
            Changed my whole life
            Me go funny on you?
            We were normal.
            Ordinary
            You were the headcases.
            The whole close
            Suffered
            From you
            Your Da
            Your mental Da
            I can still hear him
            I hear his feet
            Scraping the stairs.
            Every day
            And it's like
            Every day's
            All the one day
            That day
FRANK: What day?
CLARE: The day he fell.
KENNY: He never fell.
CLARE: He fell Kenny.
KENNY: No.
FRANK: What do you mean he never fell?
KENNY: I was stood there
            On the landing.
            He was coming up.

Pished as usual.
I'm thinking he's never going to make it
But I'm feeling sick
I can smell the midden
I didn't want him to see me
I wanted in to my house
So I'm knocking
I'm hammering on the door
But nobody answers
My mother was in
I don't know what she was doing
Then he was on the half landing
He's blind drunk.
Looking at me
'Frankie Boy'
He's saying
He wasn't scraping any more
He was coming
Every step
He was getting bigger
And I'm saying
'I'm not your boy
I'm Kenny
From one up'
He's nearly here
You shout up from the back court
He flickers
Puts his hand on the wall and misses the stair
I shut my eyes and wish
I wish hard
But he's righting himself
Him
The wall
The stair
All coming thegether
But it's a close thing
You shout again
I say
Again
'I'm not your boy'
He says something
But it's all spit

I say
'Keep away
But he keeps coming
'I mean it'
He's still coming
I hear a voice whispering
'Push him
Push him'
So
So I put out my hand
Hardly even call it a push
A tap more like
I hardly touch him
He reaches for the wall
But it's not there
And the stairs are not there either
So he's
Dead still
In mid air
For a fraction
He's going to fall on me
So I put out my other hand
And I push
Hard
Both hands
And he falls
Back
Back and down
I think
He's going to get to the half landing
And then
Get up and kill me
But he doesn't
He keeps on going
Falling and thudding and bouncing off the walls
Then
Nothing
You
Playing out the back
I know he's not going to get up now
And I'm so
Relieved I nearly pee myself

The boy upstairs calls down the close for his Dad.
It echoes.

How was I to know
You were going to
Miss him?

Something falls into place for Frank.

FRANK: You said he fell.
            You told me he fell.
CLARE: *I* said he fell.
            Kenny was sick.
FRANK: So you did.
CLARE: I was up the stairs
FRANK: So you were.
CLARE: Looking for you.
FRANK: Looking
            And whispering
            Eh?
            Was that you that was whispering?
            The wee voice
            'Push him
            Push him.'
CLARE: I don't know.
FRANK: What?
KENNY: What?
FRANK: How can you not know?
            Of course you know.
CLARE: No.
            Because
            I did
            Think it.
            I was thinking it that hard that
            I might have said it
            Out loud.   I don't know
            I swear
            Sometimes I think things
            So hard
            That I don't know if I've said them or not
            Does that never happen to you?
KENNY: I hear things
            I don't know if they're real.

62

FRANK: You pushed my Da
            Down the close stairs
            He fractured his skull
            And died
            Three days later.
            Fucking
            Don't know what's real.

Upstairs a baby cries.

FRANK: You should have told me before.
            I've spent
            All these years
            Believing in
            Justice
            And Right. So Wrong as well
            And I don't know how to look now
            Have I been seeing things that aren't really there?
            Not seeing things that
            Are there?
            Eh?
            You two
            Fucking
            Hiding
            Half my life
            What else?
            I'm scared to ask.
            Don't tell me.
            I'd have been better off
            Blind.
KENNY: Deaf.

Frank and Kenny see each other the way they are.
And they don't mind.

FRANK: I don't really miss him.
            Not how he was then. But I do miss
            Getting stronger than him
            Showing him
            Making him
            Behave.
            Thinking that

63

Maybe one day
He'd get old
And we could all just
Calm down.
The rest is
Never never.
Maybe there was
Nothing
In him to like. Maybe
I'm looking for that.
I *am* looking for that.
Because
I see a resemblance
She's right
You're right, Clare.
I look like him
A bit
I do
But I'm not
I am not
Like him
Eh?
I fight
The odd
Angry fight.
Drink
Who doesn't?
But not the way he did.
Eh?
Can you not see it?

Upstairs the boy rolls some marbles across the floor.

CLARE: You can't just show up
           With that face
           After this long time
           And say you're different.
KENNY: Yes
           Yes he can.
           Because he is.
           I can see it.
           I know his face.

	And I think he's right.
	He's different.
	We need to get out.
	We're too
	Close
	In here.
	Eh?
	Get out for a bit.
	A new light.
	That's what we need
	To see things
	In a new light.
	What do you say?
FRANK:	Aye.
	Aye.
KENNY:	Clare?
CLARE:	Sure.
	Yea.
	You two
	Go for a pint.
	That's what to do.
KENNY:	Us two?
CLARE:	Yea.
	You're fine.
	It'll be good.
FRANK:	Are you in the huff?
CLARE:	No.
	I swear.
KENNY:	She's okay.
FRANK:	You're in the huff.
	You've never changed.
	Look at you.
	What is it?
CLARE:	Nothing.
FRANK:	What?
CLARE:	Nothing.
FRANK:	Come on.
CLARE:	What is
	Going for a pint, Frank?
	It's
	Talk.
	Visions.

                    I can't do that
                    The now

Clare can't trust herself to speak to him.
She can barely look at him.

FRANK: Fuck's sake Clare
                    You look as if you've got a broken heart
                    Or something
                    I'm the one that/You could look
                    A wee bit more
                    Cheerful
                    Eh?
                    Are you greetin?
CLARE: No
                    I am not.
FRANK: Well what's that?
CLARE: Juice.
                    I've got juicy eyes.
                    Have you never noticed?
                    Don't smile at me.
FRANK: I always smile at people.
                    I'm known for my smile.
CLARE: Are you?
FRANK: Because I'm like that.
                    I'm sunny natured.
CLARE: Good.
                    That's good.
                    That's definitely different.
FRANK: See.
KENNY: I'm punctual.
                    People expect me to be on time.
FRANK: Kenny.
                    What are you doing?
KENNY: It's hard to say
                    Because
                    For a long time
                    I've been protecting Clare
                    Well
                    Myself actually
                    And hiding Clare
                    And what she's hiding

Yes
From you
And that was right
Because you were
Bad for each other
You don't know
So don't say anything
But now
I see you're eight again
And I don't want anybody to hurt you.

FRANK: Well
Who would hurt me?
Who would hurt me more than you?
Stealing my past.
That hurts me.
Lying for twenty years
That takes my breath away
But you
You're like my brother
You looked out for me.

KENNY: Yes I did.
I do.
You think you've changed
I think he has
But you haven't got older Frank
You've got younger
You're the Frankie
That lay under my bed
Making plans.
Look at you
Standing there
Talking about a boy
And being real
It's good
I never thought I'd see it again.
Did you Clare?
Did you?

CLARE: No.

KENNY: Okay then.
See.
So
And he's looking for things

	To get better
	A new life
	That should be possible
	Eh?
	For Frank.
CLARE:	Yes.
KENNY:	Good
	That's good then
	A pint well
CLARE:	One pint
FRANK:	A couple.
KENNY:	Whatever.
	See?
	Just the thought of
	Fresh air
	And I can breathe
	Easy.

Kenny makes for the door.

FRANK:	And maybe
	Over a couple of pints
	Clare can tell me
	Her dream.
	See.
	I haven't forgotten.
KENNY:	No
	Frank.
	We were nearly there.
	Nearly out the door.
	You don't want to start all that.
	Dreams.
	What are they?
	Get you nowhere.
FRANK:	No
	No
	I'm all for dreams
	Long as you know what they mean.
	And I kind of
	Cut Clare off
	Not intentionally
	But

	I had to get things straight
	So now
	It's only fair.
	Eh?
CLARE:	No.
	Kenny's right.
	And anyway
	I couldn't
	Now.
KENNY:	There we are then.
FRANK:	Hiding
	Don't
	Eh?
	I've had enough of that.
KENNY:	Look.
	It's no big deal.
	She told me.
	I'll tell you
	She had a dream about the boy/A
	Boy
	And it was a nice dream
	He had a face
	So she was happy
FRANK:	That's it?
KENNY:	That's it.
	A happy dream.
	Let it be.
FRANK:	Something else.
	Look at her face.
KENNY:	Fix your face Clare.
	Jesus
	Will you just/
FRANK:	Do you not know anything yet
	Kenny?
CLARE:	No
	He's right
	That was my dream
	About the boy
	And it was
	A happy dream.

Upstairs the boy hums.

CLARE:	But it's not the one I usually have.
	Your dream about a boy
	I don't know how it came to you
	I have this one all the time
	And usually it's the same thing
	A boy on his daddy's shoulders.
	I see them at the dump
	Putting bottles in the skip
FRANK:	I would do that.
	See
	Nobody ever did that with me.
CLARE:	No.
	I know.
	And he's singing
	'Ten green bottles
	Accidentally fall'
	Smash.
	I'm watching
	And smiling
	You know how you know you're smiling in a
	dream
	But something's keeping me there
	I think it's the bottles.
	I'm waiting for him to finish
	Putting all the bottles in the bin
	And then I can go
	But he finishes
	And his daddy starts to turn round
	And I look at the boy's face
	He has such a nice voice
	And he turns
	And it's blank
	His face is blank
	And suddenly I'm in a horror film
	Because it's not just
	Blank
	It's like it's been burnt.
	And it flies through the air and sticks to my face
	I can't breathe for it
	And then I wake up
	Breathless.
FRANK:	That's a fucking
	Nightmare.

KENNY:	You never told me that.
CLARE:	No.
KENNY:	But today
	You said/
CLARE:	Yes.
	Today, Frank
	This morning
FRANK:	This morning
CLARE:	Today when I dreamt it
	He had a face.
FRANK:	I'm relieved.
	I feel the relief for you.
CLARE:	Eyes
	Nose
	Mouth
	A proper face.
FRANK:	Whose face?
CLARE:	That was the question.
	Your face, Frank
FRANK:	And then I turned up.
CLARE:	It's the only face he could've had.
KENNY:	It couldn't have been my face.
	Clare has never loved me like that.
CLARE:	That's not it.
	All these years, Frank.
	I've kept you out there.
	Hiding behind Kenny
	I was scared.
FRANK:	Scared of me?
CLARE:	Something.
	Scared to look at you.
	I know every bit of your face, Frank.
	And I can see you
	As a boy
	A beautiful wee boy
	With tufty hair
	And a screwed up face.
	And I know that
	Because/And you're right
	All this hiding
	Going on
	I should have been scared

	For you
	Not me
	Because
	I had your boy.
	I had your boy and I
	Gave him away.
	And I never told you.
	The last time I saw him
	He was screaming blue murder.
	He had all his fingers and toes.
FRANK:	The skin
	Has just fell off my ribs
	And they're dissolving
	Inside my gut
	No
	No
	Kenny
	Come on
	What's the game?
KENNY:	No game
	Me
	Hiding her
	Hiding him
	That's it.
	Frank
	You were/
FRANK:	Don't.
	Don't.
	Ah fuck.
	Ah fuck.
	I'm my Da
	I am
	I'm
	Falling down the stairs
	Banging off the walls.
CLARE:	They were
	Nice people.
	Professional.
	I had nothing.
FRANK:	You had me.
CLARE:	I didn't.
	We weren't even/I was fifteen.

	You were screwing Marie Kelly.
FRANK:	So you gave my boy away?
CLARE:	I didn't know you'd want him.
FRANK:	I didn't
	Then.
	But I do now.
CLARE:	Look at you Frank
	You're a bar man.
	You drink.
	You're always skint.
	You're nearly forty and you've decided you've
	Been around long enough
	So the next thing is
	You want a boy.
	Too late.
	I was a mess.
	You want to know about mothers
	Here's mine
	Hand raised
	Tongue between her teeth
	Ready to leather me
	Because I stole her life
	I couldn't do that
	I couldn't take that chance
	With the boy
	They were good people.
	They really wanted him.
FRANK:	They wanted a baby.
	What about when he gets bigger?
	What if he's bad?
	What if he's like me?
	Or my Da?
	They won't know that.
	They won't know how to love him
	If he's bad.
	They'll try to punish it out of him.
	All these years
	Twenty years.
	He could be a real mess.

Upstairs the man yells at the boy.
Slaps.

They all hear it.

FRANK: Look at me.
                 Look at my ugly face.
                 I've been avoiding this face.
                 I saw it on my Da.
                 I thought
                 I'm never having that face
                 And look
                 Here it is.
                 Stuck to me.
                 Don't look at me.
                 Don't look at me.

They all face away from each other.

FRANK: I can't even look for him.
                 Can I?
                 No.
                 No way.
                 He'll think I'm a bum.
                 He'll think
                 Who's the drunk?
                 Why the fuck
                 Would anybody
                 Get into that state?
                 He won't see
                 That I'm peaking.
                 That this is my time.
KENNY: And you are.
                 It is.
                 I see it.
                 Definitely.
FRANK: Don't look at me.
KENNY: I'm not looking.
FRANK: *(to Clare)* Turn away.
                 I don't want you to look at me.
CLARE: You look like your boy.
                 Not your Da
                 I bet he's got your smile
                 I bet he has.
FRANK: Has he?

74

	In your dream
	Was he smiling?
	Was he?
CLARE:	Yes
	Yes he was
	He looked
	Sunny natured.
FRANK:	That's something then
	Eh?
CLARE:	Something.
FRANK:	Your back is the length of my arm.
	I bet you never knew that.
CLARE:	Your face is the width of my hand.

Upstairs the boy runs across the floor.
Kenny looks up.

KENNY:	Shoosh wee boy.
	Shoosh.

An Instant Playscript

Riddance first published in Great Britain in 1999 as
a paperback original by Nick Hern Books Limited,
14 Larden Road, London W3 7ST
in association with Paines Plough

Typeset by Country Setting, Kingsdown, Kent CT14 8ES
Printed and bound in Great Britain

ISBN 1 85459 465 6

A CIP catalogue record for this book is available from
the British Library